Assembly Points

100 Short Points
for School Assemblies

Rod & Scott Whiteley

MOORLEY'S Print & Publishing

British Library Cataloguing in Publication Data.
A catalogue record for this book is available
from the British Library.

ISBN 0 86071 545 0

MOORLEY'S Print & Publishing
23 Park Rd., Ilkeston, Derbys DE7 5DA
✂ Tel/Fax: (0115) 932 0643 ✂

Foreword

Assembly points is a collection of short stories and thought starters to illustrate ideals for living to primary school children. Each of the tales can be built into an already planned assembly or be the starting point for a new one. Themes include pulling together, sharing, sportsmanship, patience, respect and honesty.

The stories are written in children's language, with modern day issues youngsters can relate to. They can be dramatised, and are meant to be 'told' rather than read.

1 A farmer tied two horses together, back to back and left them on a track between two fields.

One of them was hungry. He tried to pull the other towards the field nearest to him.

The second horse was also hungry. He pulled towards 'his' field. It was like a 'tug of war.'

Neither could pull the other to the grass. They soon became tired.

The first horse said, "Let's stop pulling against each other and work together."

They walked side by side and ate the grass in the first field.

Later they turned round and walked to the second field.

They enjoyed another meal.

The horses learned to live <u>together</u>.

2 Marco should not have been near the airport runway.

He was very hungry waiting for a plane full of food to land.

A biscuit dropped on the floor as the plane was unloaded. When nobody was watching, Marco crawled across the runway and put the biscuit in his pocket. It was more than he'd eaten for two days.

He was about to go when the pilot got out of the plane. Marco asked him for some money. The pilot said he hadn't any. Marco asked again.

The pilot turned his pockets inside out.

When he saw they were empty, Marco felt sorry for him.

Marco took the biscuit out of his pocket, broke it in two and gave half to the pilot.

Marco was prepared to share his food with somebody else even though he was hungry.

Would you do the same?

3 'Old Sam' was on his way home from the market carrying two heavy bags when he tripped up. He cut his arm. Fruit and vegetables fell on the pavement. Some teenagers saw it happen.

They kicked him, stole his shopping and wallet and ran away. God was watching. He was not happy. He had an action replay.

Sam fell again. The teenagers did not kick him, but they stole the shopping and the wallet and ran off. God was still not happy. He had another action replay.

Sam fell again. The teenagers didn't harm him. They helped him to his feet, picked up his shopping and left. God still wasn't happy. He had a final action replay.

Sam fell again. The teenagers didn't hurt him. They helped him up, repacked his shopping and carried it home. They cleaned and bandaged his arm, and made him a cup of tea. They offered him their help if he ever needed it.

God was happy.

Action replays are in this story, and on 'Match of the day.' They are not part of real life. We need to do as God wishes the first time.

4 Repeat the final action replay from the previous assembly.

Today's story can be mimed to music.

One day a man went into a bank. He sneaked down a corridor and hit a guard on the head. He forced open a door, went into the vault room and shot three guards.

He wired explosives to the safe and blew it open. He grabbed the money and ran out shooting another guard.

Ask the children which story they liked best. They will probably say the second. Here you could shout, "I DON'T AGREE!"

"It was full of greed, violence and evil."

Why was yesterday's story better?

5 Tommy came home from school one day. He asked his mother if he could go to his friend's birthday party. He wanted to wear his new grey trousers, jumper and shirt. She agreed, as long as he didn't get them dirty.

Tommy promised to be home at 7.30pm.

On the day of the party, Tommy went to school in his new clothes. He came home at 4.30pm. He opened the back door quietly, tiptoed through the hall and went upstairs. He hoped Mum hadn't seen him.

Mum heard the door creak. She asked him what he was doing. She couldn't believe it. Tommy was covered from head to foot in mud. Mum was very cross. She told him to go straight to bed after cleaning himself.

At 7 o'clock Dad arrived. Tommy heard Mum tell him what had happened. He sounded very upset. Dad came upstairs, and went into his room. Tommy pretended to snore.

Dad knew he wasn't asleep. He said, "You've got two minutes to tell me what happened. You promised not to ruin your new clothes. You disobeyed your Mum. If I'm not satisfied with your answer I'll punish you."

Tommy found it difficult to speak. "It's these boys in my class. They don't like me because I'm a Christian. They don't believe in Jesus. They tease me for following him and going to Sunday School."

Dad looked puzzled. He asked Tommy what this had to do with his clothes.

Tommy explained. "Outside school there is a board with a picture of Jesus on it. It says, 'I am the way, the truth and the life.' The boys didn't like it. They wanted one advertising Manchester United, with Ryan Giggs wearing Reebok boots. They wanted to spoil it. I thought they were joking. They weren't. They threw stones at it. I was upset. I couldn't stand it, Dad. I put my arms out to protect Jesus. They hit me. I didn't mind because I was stopping him getting hurt."

Dad asked Tommy to remove his shirt. His body was covered in blood and bruises. Dad was horrified. He said, "I'm not going to punish you. I shall report the boys to the head teacher. I am proud you were brave enough to stand up for Jesus."

6 Premier League football is on television almost seven days a week.

How many armchair viewers watch a live amateur or schoolboy match?

The younger the team, the more likely they are to chase the ball. They try to kick it .... not the man. Words spoken are mostly of praise and encouragement.

This is not so with adults. Big wages bring a 'Win-at-all-costs' attitude. Bad language is used to put players off. This shouldn't be part of any sport.

One day, Arsenal played Everton. Alan Ball ran down the wing towards two defenders. They swore at him to put him off. Ignoring them, he used his skills, dribbled past and crossed the ball for Joe Royle to score.

Alan Ball let his feet do the talking.

God gave us different talents. Speed, skill, strength, stamina and determination.

These are more than enough to win any match.

'Cheats never beat!'

<table>
<tr><td>

7

</td><td>

I hope you can remember our assembly, 'Cheats never beat.'

</td></tr>
</table>

Everyone has felt the pain of iodine on a sore wound.

At the local cricket club, when a player was hurt, Fred hobbled onto the field with a case of creams and potions - from Dettol to 'Fiery Jack.' Whatever the injury, he always rubbed on the cream which stung the most!

Players leapt to their feet long before he reached them. The thought of a sharp pain brought a quick recovery.

Similarly, on local football pitches 'injured' players jump up at the sight of the trainer's bucket - the threat of the 'cold sponge' over their heads, or down their backs makes them get up.

Those who pretend to be injured - by diving - in the modern game are sent off for tricking the referee and getting other players into trouble.

There are enough '<u>real</u>' injuries in sport without 'play actors.'

They could do with a dose of Fred's fiercest potion!

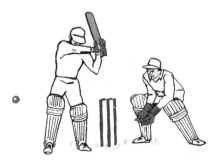

8

I hate traffic lights!

For years I have tried to be patient waiting at a red light knowing those crossing my path are happy they can go.

I remain impatient.

I need to remember the fable of the two walkers who met on a narrow mountain path. Both refused to go back to a place wide enough for them to pass. Their impatience led to anger. They tried to push each other out of the way and fell to their death.

If they had waited a minute longer they would have seen two mountain goats meet on the same path. One laid down, the other stepped gently over. They parted friends and went safely on their way.

We can all learn from mountain goats!

9 Michael 'Eddie the Eagle' Edwards was a British ski jumper. He was famous for coming last most of the time. He normally only jumped half the distance of the winner.

Eddie became famous. The press laughed at his efforts. They felt he was an embarrassment to the British team.

If on holiday in Austria, visit the Olympic stadium at Innsbruck. Climb to the top of the ski jump. Look down. You will be amazed how steep the ramp is. I wouldn't jump for anything!

Eddie did - <u>and</u> he landed on his feet.

Eddie was braver than me. He deserved his moment of fame.

Winning isn't everything.

10 Simon and Andrew were brothers. They argued a lot. They fell out over who should fetch the milk for mum, TV programmes, and games.

Mum was tired of the boys arguing. On Simon's birthday, she baked a cake. She invited his friends for tea.

After the party there was some cake left. Mum knew what would happen.

The boys began to argue. Both made a grab for the cake. Mum stopped them. She said, "Simon, you <u>cut</u> the cake, Andrew you choose which piece you want <u>first</u>."

Simon sliced the cake carefully. He wanted to make sure his brother didn't get the biggest bit. He cut it down the middle. Andrew looked at the two pieces. They were exactly the same.

The brothers began to learn to share things <u>equally</u>.

11 Peter and his friends built a snowman.

When they finished, the boys pulled their sledges to the top of the hill and raced down. At 5 o'clock, everyone went home for tea except Peter. He wanted another go.

He pushed his sledge faster than ever and jumped on.

Halfway down the hill, the sledge hit a rock buried in the snow. Peter was thrown off. He cut his head. No one saw what happened --- except the snowman! He went to Peter and gently lifted him up.

The snowman carried Peter to a rescue hut. He put him on a bed, cleaned and bandaged his head. He saw Peter was shivering. He did something a snowman should never do. He lit a fire!

As the fire warmed the hut, Peter stopped shivering. However, the snowman began to melt. First his head, then his body until there was nothing left except a pool of water.

When he didn't come home for tea, Peter's Mum went looking for him. She found the sledge and followed the trail to the hut. As she opened the door, Peter sat up feeling much better.

I wonder if she knew how Peter got there?

The snowman gave his life to save Peter.

12 Tony said his prayers every night. His parents said God always listened.

One day he went to the zoo. He liked all the animals. His favourites were the lion cubs.

That night in his prayers, Tony asked for a lion cub on his birthday.

Mum and Dad hoped he would forget. He didn't. They didn't know what to do. Tony was sure God would answer.

On his birthday, he was excited as dad gave him a box with fur sticking out. He opened it. Inside there was a ....kitten!

"You said God always listens to my prayers!" he cried.

"He does," said Dad.

"Sometimes he says NO."

(Ask the children why they think God said no.)

It's not always possible to always get what you ask for. Lions are not pets!

13

Frankie was cruel.

He saw a bird fly into a tree and break its wing. He picked the bird up, broke its other wing and threw it in the pond. The bird drowned. Frankie thought it was funny.

He saw a cat with its head stuck in a tin. He picked the cat up by its tail and threw it in some nettles. The cat squealed in pain. Frankie laughed.

He saw a dog with a thorn in its paw. He cut a stick from the thorn bush and hit it. It was hurt badly. Frankie giggled. He thought it was clever.

God was watching. He was very upset. He decided to teach Frankie a lesson. He made him have a dream.

In the dream Frankie was the bird, the cat and the dog. The cruel things were done to him.

"Now you know how it feels," said God.

Frankie did not think it was funny.

(Ask the children: 'How would Frankie treat each creature now he had learnt his lesson?')

14 Bill Roberts worked down the pit all his life.

The young miners did not appreciate his experience. He was a slow worker. His pace stopped them getting their bonus.

They wanted him moved. The boss refused.

Two weeks later the roof fell in trapping the miners. They screamed and shouted, pulling at the fallen rocks.

Bill told them to sit down and stop panicking. They were using up precious oxygen. He began to calm them down by telling jokes. Every so often Bill told the men to tap their feet.

He started a game of cards. He held a quiz, asked them to recall holiday memories and led a sing-song. They tapped at regular intervals.

After six hours they heard tapping of a different kind. It was a rescue team!

Later, a young miner was asked what it was like to be trapped for six hours.

"Six hours!" he said, "It seemed like six minutes. Bill kept our minds off the danger. He saved our lives. If it hadn't been for his experience in sending the tapping messages, the rescue team wouldn't have known where we were and if we were alive."

Older people's experience and wisdom are often vital - not just down a mine.

15	Tony: "Alan there's a boy outside - he's upset."
	Alan: *(Youth Leader)* "Bring him in."

Tony: "Here he is. He's called Scott."

Alan: "Hello Scott, what's the matter?"

Scott: "It's my Dad. I hate him.
(Picks up brick - being used as a goalpost - in his right hand.)
I could throw this at him. He's always telling me what to do. I've run away."

Alan: "You've got a bag. What's in it? A toothbrush? Pyjamas? Clothes? A Game Boy?"

(Scott shows Alan a CD, game, ball and holds a cross in his left hand.)

Alan: "What's that?"

Scott: "The cross of Jesus."

Alan: "What does it mean?"

Scott: "The love Jesus gave when he died for us."

Alan: "Throw it in the bin. It's no good to you!"

Scott: "Why not? We should love each other."

(Alan holds brick and cross)

Alan: "You can't hold love in one hand and hate in the other. You said you hate your Dad <u>and</u> we should love one another. Make your mind up. What happened at home?"

Scott: "I asked for a racing bike. Dad said I was too small. I have to wait a year."

Alan: "He said it because he loves you. He didn't want you to be killed in an accident. I'll take you home later. Your dad will be pleased to see you."

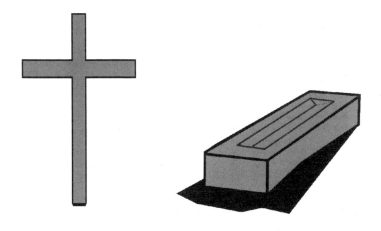

16 A quarter of the world has too much to eat. Three quarters is starving.

A gardener had a snail race. The winner could have anything he wanted.

The race lasted three hours!

Terry was the winner. When asked what he would like for his 'prize' he said, "I want to be the only snail that can eat in the vegetable patch."

His friends wanted a share. Terry kept it for himself.

Terry ate and ate and ate. He did not see what was happening to his friends.

One day he saw Peter, his best friend lying on the floor. He had died of starvation.

"What have I done?" said Terry realising how greedy and selfish he had been.

If we don't share our food with poorer countries, millions of people will die.

17 Mr Jones was the manager in a racing car factory. He was friendly and helpful to the workers.

On Saturday the men went to the racetrack. They wanted 'their' car to win. It never did. The owner wanted to know why. One of the workers, Mr Adams told him.

"It's Mr Jones, he's too soft with the men. If I was the manager, I would make them work much harder."

The owner sacked Mr Jones. He wanted to win badly. He appointed Mr Adams. The men were upset with the way he bullied them. They wanted Mr Jones back. When the manager said 'NO', they made a plan.

The men made a car which was safe but slow. In the next race it came last. The owner was angry. He wanted to know why the car was slower than ever. The men explained. They said, "Mr Jones is kind and listens to us. Mr Adams is a bully."

The owner brought back Mr Jones. The men were so pleased to see him, they made their best racing car ever. It came first!

We respond better to encouragement.

18 Alison wanted to talk about Jesus. There were lots of things she didn't understand. She asked Dad. He said, "He died to save us and help people live a good and clean life."

Alison was still unsure. Dad took her to the seaside to help explain things.

When the sea went out, Dad gave Alison a stick. He told her to write as many bad words as she could think of in the sand.

She wrote; kill, steal, cheat, bully and hurt.

(Can you think of any others?)

When she finished, Dad said,
"Look at the words carefully. Lots of people do these things every day." He paused. "Now watch and wait," he said.

The tide came in and washed away the words. In the morning the beach was clean. Dad said, "That's what Jesus did for us. He died so all the wrong things <u>we do</u> can be wiped away."

| 19 | Many older people think a play station is where a toy electric train stops. Today the 'Playstation' is a high performance action game console. |

The games are fast, exciting and fun.

The 'Playstation' and games cost a lot of money. They teach you to think quickly and use skills needed to work a computer, drive a car and even fly a plane.

Ryan was tired of being told what to do. He was fed up of people saying things like. "Ryan, tidy your room." "No you can't, you're not old enough yet."

He wanted to prove there were things he could do better than them.

One night he challenged Dad to a game of Tomb Raider III. Dad didn't get past the first stage. Ryan completed the mission. He guided Lara safely through the different dangers. He was delighted.

Older people have a lot of knowledge, skill and advice to pass on. We should listen to them.

Young people can also pass on things they have learnt.

Share your talents with somebody else.

One day a lion started to boast.

He said: "I'm the king of the jungle, nobody dare challenge me!"

None of the animals dared to.

When the mosquito challenged him, the lion laughed. As he did, his mouth opened wide. The mosquito flew inside and stung him - again and again!

In great pain the lion shouted: "You win! I give in!"

Soon the mosquito started to boast.

"I'm the king of the jungle! I beat the lion!"

He was so busy showing off he didn't look where he was going. He flew into a spider's web.

The spider gobbled him up!

Pride comes before a fall.

| 21 |

Mr Fox heard the dogs chasing him!

He ran for his life. He leaped across a stream and hid in a cave. He pulled rocks over the front and kept very still.

While he was hiding, he said to his ears: "You are no use, I'll throw you away."

"You wouldn't have heard the dogs without us," said his ears.

He said to his legs: "You are no use, I'll throw you away."

They replied: "You couldn't have run away and jumped over the stream without us."

He said to his eyes: "You are no use, I'll throw you away."

They said: "Without us you wouldn't have seen the cave."

He said to his tail: "You are no use I'll throw you away."
"I wiped your footprints away," said his tail.

He said to his nose: "You are no use, I'll throw you away."

His nose did not reply. Mr Fox stuck his nose out of the cave. One of the dogs bit it sharply!

He could not smell for a week.

He realised every part of his body was important.

Which parts were not in the story?

Which part of your body is the most important?

Sally's headmaster asked her to paint a big picture. It would take a year to finish if she worked one afternoon a week.

Sally's friends watched her paint. They liked the colours, shapes and patterns.

Sally knew her friends often smoked, took drugs, got drunk and stayed up all night. She tried to stop them. They ignored her. Sally wanted to change them.

One day she began to tear the picture into pieces. Her friends told her to stop. They didn't want her to ruin it. Sally said; "That's what you're doing with your life."

Sally's friends took notice. They began to change.

Is there anything you can change?

23 Have you ever been tempted to steal?

Ian's Mum and Dad were out. He went to their bedroom and searched the cupboards and drawers.

He found an envelope with £200 in it.

He wanted to buy a computer game. He was sure they wouldn't miss £10.

A month later it was his birthday. He came downstairs and opened his cards. The one from his Mum and Dad had a mountain bike on the front.

Inside was a note. It read:
>   The mountain bike we'd chosen you costs £200.
>   We couldn't buy it because we were £10 short.

Ian never stole again.

24 Anne was given a new game called, 'The Countryside Code'.

In the first part she had to break it.

She took a short cut instead of sticking to the path. She went through a gate and left it open. After a picnic she dropped litter.

She scored 10 penalty points for killing the crops. She scored 15 penalty points for letting the sheep out of the open gate. She scored 20 penalty points when a cow choked eating a plastic bag.

Anne was shocked at the results.

In part two she was asked to keep the code.

What did she do differently?

(Teachers may like to include other parts of the countryside code.)

25	God gave us different strengths.

He set a test for Mr Large, Mr Medium and Mr Small.

They were sent on a journey.

Whilst climbing a mountain they came to a big gap. Mr Large made a human bridge. Mr Medium and Mr Small walked safely across.

Later the wind blew their map into a tiny cave. Mr Small crawled inside to fetch it.

Near the end of the journey they came to a deep river. They had to make a raft to cross it.

Mr Large sat at one end and Mr Small at the other. The raft began to tip over! It's a good job Mr Medium was with them. He sat with Mr Small to balance it.

God was pleased. They had used their different strengths to help complete the journey.

26

Have you ever lost your temper?

Angela wanted to be a waitress. A café gave her a trial.

The manager asked her to take orders. There were 12 people sat at 3 tables.

The first 4 were served in 10 minutes. Angela gave their food with a smile.

The second tables meal took 20 minutes. They complained. Angela said sorry and smiled.

The third set were served in 30 minutes. They shouted at her.

Angela didn't blame the chef. She didn't grumble. She smiled, apologised, and offered to fetch the manager.

He came with a big smile. He had set Angela a test. He said: "You stayed calm and kept smiling. Others might have lost their temper. The job is yours!

27 Peter was happy and healthy.

One day he was playing football when suddenly he collapsed.

He was rushed to hospital. The doctors said he'd damaged his lungs.

Peter needed new ones quickly.

Sam was riding his bike. A car flew round a corner and killed him.

After looking at Sam, the doctors realised his lungs could be used to help Peter.

Sam's parents were upset. They didn't know what to do.

They went to see Peter. He was very poorly.

There was only one thing they could do.

Sam's lungs saved Peter's life.

28 Mr Thompson owned a toyshop.

He sold toys to children who promised to look after them.

Jordan bought an Action man, a racing car and a dragon.

He said he would take care of them.

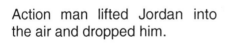

Jordan treated the toys badly. They were soon chipped and broken.

One night he had a dream.

The toys had a meeting. Action man said: "I'm tired of being thrown about."

The dragon cried: "I'm sick of him pulling my wings and tail."

The racing car driver decided: "We need to teach him a lesson."

Action man lifted Jordan into the air and dropped him.

The racing car knocked him down.

The dragon breathed fire over him!

Jordan was glad to wake up.

He learned not to break his promise, or the toys again.

29 It was Christmas day. Billy was excited.

Mum and Dad bought him a puppy. He called him Scrappy.

Billy took him for long walks. He brushed Scrappy, fed him, and kept him clean.

After 4 weeks, Billy couldn't be bothered taking Scrappy out. He stopped feeding and washing him.

Scrappy had to be taken back. Mum was cross.

She had always washed and ironed Billy's football kit and cleaned his boots.

One day Billy came home covered in mud.

It was raining outside. Mum threw his things out.

His kit was ruined, and his boots cracked.

On the shirt was a photo of Scrappy.

On the back it read: 'I couldn't be bothered!'

30 The roads were dug up. The water had been turned off.

Dad was annoyed: "I can't water the garden!"

Mum was furious: "I can't cook the tea."

Annie was fuming: "I can't have a shower."

Jody was cross: "I can't wash my car!"

The family ordered a takeaway.

They watched the news headlines.

"Ethiopia in trouble. No water for 18 months. Hundreds dying."

They looked at each other.

".......and we complained about not having water for one day."

31 Dave was in prison hospital. He was very poorly.

The Vicar came to visit. He said: "Can I do anything?"

Dave replied: "Let's play noughts and crosses. Can I be noughts?"

It was 5 games all and the vicar's turn.

X	O	X
O		O
X	O	X

He refused - "You finish it."

Dave looked confused. He put the 0 in and asked: "Why did you let me win?"

The vicar rubbed out the crosses. "Jesus died so our sins might be forgiven."

Dave looked at the cross of circles.

	O	
O	O	O
	O	

He began to cry. "Am I too late?"

 The vicar put the paper in Dave's hand and said: "It's never too late."

37

32 Jimmy, Rich and Corky were always fighting.

The teachers tried to stop them; "No break time, football or trips."

It didn't work.

Mr Morris was fed up. He asked them why they did it.

Jimmy said: "Soccer and rugby players fight on the television."

Rich boasted: "My Granddad did it in the war."

Corky shouted: "My Dad says I've to stick up for myself!"

Mr Morris nodded - he had an idea.

He invited three guests to school assembly.

A rugby player with cauliflower ears and crooked teeth.

A soldier who had one eye and no legs.

A boxer with a bent nose and who couldn't speak properly.

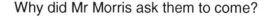

Why did Mr Morris ask them to come?

33

Mr Thompson opened the door.

Outside was a man with a ring in his nose.

He said: "I'm collecting for orphans."

Mr Thompson took one look and closed the door.

A month later he watched an awards programme.

It showed the top charities in the area.

Number ten was for work with the blind.

Mr Thompson lost interest till it came to number one.

Pictures of abandoned children in Romania made him cry.

A big lorry was shown full of toys for the orphans.

The driver was Michael Simms.

The name didn't mean anything to Mr Thompson.

The nose ring did.

> Don't judge people by their appearance.

34 The king dressed in disguise.

He went round the country.

He was disappointed.

People were swearing, lying, stealing and being cruel.

He said: "Stop it!"

No one took any notice.

He tried again.

A man argued: "You can't tell us what to do!"

The king went back to his castle to think.

He asked his servants to call the people together.

He told them: "You need to change."

"How do you know?" shouted a man.

He put the disguise back on.

"I've <u>seen</u> the way you behave."

We can't see God, but he's there.

35 Mr Vole was hungry.

He searched for a morning snack.

He spotted some blackberries but couldn't reach them.

He tried jumping and climbing.

Mr Butterfly laughed as he ate them. "You'll never get up here without wings," he said.

Mr Bee grinned; "All the more for us!"

Mr Vole carried on his search. He found an elderberry bush with some fruit at low level.

A flock of birds frightened Mr Butterfly and Mr Bee away and ate the blackberries.

Mr Vole was tempted to laugh at the hungry pair.

Instead he shared his elderberries.

Two wrongs don't make a right.

Some people are afraid to use credit cards, computers and mobile phones.

They write letters but have no idea how to send an E-mail. It is hard to convince them an E-mail is faster and cheaper!

Mr and Mrs Evans were disabled. They didn't like asking friends or relatives to do their shopping.

Mark took his lab top computer to their house. He showed them how easy it was to order from the internet. They could even do their banking.

Mark helped Mr and Mrs Evans become independent again.

They were even brave enough to send Mark an E-mail to thank him!

Change has its advantages.

37

The children tuned in to a new challenge programme called 'Escape!'

Contestants were told the world would end tomorrow.

They could escape in a rocket.

Matthew went first.

When asked what he would take with him he said: "My Gameboy".

Questioned who he'd take he replied: "A robot".

His answer to where he would fly was "Mars".

Gayle chose to take the Bible and her family to Heaven.

Some of the boys in the studio audience jeered.

"What use are they? She won't win."

The rockets took off. On their journey they had to overcome different problems.

The final stage took them to a large metal gate.

A guard stood outside. He said: "Are you escaping from earth?"

"I can't let you in unless you have brought, Love, Faith and Happiness."

He let Gayle in.

Matthew had to turn back.

38 Judy's Grandma put a used bottle on the table.

She said: "There is a picture of life – What's wrong with it?"

Judy wasn't sure.

"It's empty!" said Gran.

She replaced the first one with a bottle of fresh milk.

"Now I can see a better picture of life," said Judy. "This one is full."

"…But it's only full of one thing," said Gran. "Here is the best picture."

She put a bottle full of Smarties on the table and said: "This life is full of lots of different things."

Judy got the message but I think she'd rather have had the Smarties.

39 A statue of peace was built between two countries.

It was so small they didn't notice it. They started an 'arms race'.

They built bigger and more powerful weapons.

A girl was afraid her family might be killed. She sent the countries two pictures.

A small one with 100 dead soldiers.

A large one with 1000 dead soldiers.

She pinned a note on them. It said: 'The bigger the weapons, the more soldiers will <u>die</u>!'

The message got through.

The weapons were melted and made into a bigger statue of peace.

40 Alan loved zoos.

He liked watching the animals being fed.

When he got older, he thought zoos were cruel.

He said: "God didn't make animals to be locked in a cage."

One night he broke into the zoo.

He set the animals free.

The day after he was horrified when:-

A lion killed a girl. The giraffe broke his neck going under a bridge. A bear was shot in the woods.

Luckily the other animals were soon caught.

Do <u>you</u> think zoos are cruel?

Never do what Alan did.

How could you show your feelings differently?

There were 20 seconds to go. Mandy passed to Kim.

She aimed, shot and scored.

Wichester had won the league.

The girls celebrated. They sang: "We are the champions!"

"We're the best!" shouted Joe.

The coach opened the door. She had a straight face.

She held a small bag.

She said: "I've got the names of five big time Charlies in here!"

The girls looked puzzled. No one wanted to be a 'Big time Charlie.'

Next season they won the league and cup.

The bag had motivated them to a successful double.

What motivates you?

42 The railway police came to school to show a film called: 'Robbie.'

It told the story of Robbie and his friends.

They had been playing in the park.

On the way home they took a short cut through a hole in a fence. It led to a railway line. Robbie's foot got stuck under the track. There was a horrific scream. The children in assembly were shocked and frightened.

When the film resumed, Robbie was in hospital with one foot missing.

Nigel didn't listen.

A week later he was killed on a railway line.

He had ignored Robbie's scream.

43 'Blasterman' was the new action hero on TV.

The children were quick to copy him.

They loved pretending to blast each other to pieces.

The Head Teacher was concerned these 'war games' might become violent and someone would get hurt.

He'd heard of a child in America who'd shot and killed another pupil.

One afternoon, he asked if he could join in.

The children thought it was great. They blasted him to bits.

"I need to practise," he said.

The pupils watched as he built a shooting range.

They cheered and clapped as he shot down six dummies with a pellet rifle.

One by one he replaced the dummies with cardboard replicas of six children from the school.

Would they recognise the faces before he pulled the trigger?

There was silence as he took aim.

"Stop!" they shouted.

It was the last 'Blasterman' game played at the school.

44 God doesn't help us win, but Katy believed he once did.

She entered a floral display contest.

She arranged flowers with different colours, shapes and sizes.

Katy looked at the other entries. They were all good.

She thought: "How can I make mine that little bit better?"

She went to the park gardens and hoped God might give her a clue.

She noticed the prettiest flowers were in the middle.

Katy put hers in the same place and won FIRST PRIZE!

God speaks to us in different ways.

45 Children follow different crazes, the latest being Pokemon – a furry animal with different skills and strengths.

Pupils at Woverthorpe School loved them. They liked to buy and swap cards.

Lee bought a pack. He got the strongest Pokemon.

Friends were jealous. They asked to swap. Lee refused.

They beat him up.

Mrs Maule was upset. She brought 3 large cards to school.

The first showed:- 'Muscles Pokemon' - 10 for strength, speed and skill.

The second:- 'Handsome Pokemon' - 10 for looks, fashion and appearance.

The third:- A picture of a weak bleeding man - strength and power 0.

Mrs Maule asked pupils which they'd like. They shouted:- "Muscles and Handsome."

She ripped up the cards and held the third: - "This is Jesus."

A child shouted; "Why choose him, he scores 0 for everything!"

She replied; "He gave his strength and power up for you."

Let Jesus rule your life – not a pack of cards!

46 A party of visitors were looking round a church.

They liked the peaceful atmosphere.

They enjoyed lighting a candle for a friend.

As the group were walking round, the sun shone through the stained glass windows.

Each window had a picture from the Bible except one!

It showed a man in jeans and a T-shirt sweeping the floor.

They pointed at it and said: "What's he doing there? He's got nothing to do with the Bible."

A church member walked over. She said: "That's our old caretaker Phil. He kept the building spotless for 50 years. This is how we wanted to remember him."

Jesus said: - "When you see one who does good work, you see me."

47 A drama group came into school.

They dressed in party clothes and danced to loud music.

Spike pulled people into a corner and offered them tablets.

Mike was tempted.

He swallowed a tablet. It made him feel great.

He danced all night. Mike had never had so much fun.

The next morning he was violently sick. His heart pounded quickly.

He sweated a lot. He felt depressed.

Mike couldn't face talking

– not even to Mum and Dad.

48

If you make a mistake – do you put it right?

A platoon of soldiers were captured.

The sergeant wanted to show the enemy his men were disciplined.

The enemy leader shouted: "Build me a bridge across the river!"

The sergeant was determined his men would complete the job.

"Let's show them we can do it!" he ordered.

He didn't realise the bridge was being built to carry enemy weapons and troops.

A group of men planned to blow up the bridge.

The sergeant spotted the wire and the dynamite.

The men fired shots at him.

They didn't want him to ruin the mission.

The sergeant realised his mistake. He cried: "What have I done?"

Wounded and in agony he set the dynamite off.

He blew up the bridge.

We remember him because he corrected his error.

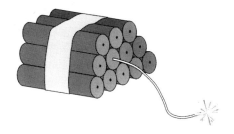

49 It's important to train properly.

The pilots were lowered into a dinghy.

A big wave threw it onto some rocks.

The oars were lost, and water gushed through a hole.

The pilots panicked and jumped over board.

They watched this on video. The trainer said: "If the rescue helicopter hadn't been there – you would have drowned." Think first!

They started again.

The same thing happened.

This time the pilots kept calm, plugged the hole and baled out the water.

They paddled to safety with their hands.

If their plane crash landed in the sea, they would know what to do.

50 'Changed people change people.'

Vic was a criminal. He was sent to prison.

On release he returned to crime. He was soon back in a cell.

One morning he saw a photograph in the paper. It was his Granddad.

His nose was smashed to pieces and he was blinded in one eye.

He had been attacked by robbers.

Vic was horrified. It made him think about what he'd done.

He changed into a different man. He wanted to help other prisoners.

Vic pinned some pictures on the prison notice board.

The first showed his Granddad with an arm round his grandson. Both were smiling and content.

The second pictured Vic as a criminal.

The third showed Granddad's battered face.

The prisoners were shocked at what had happened to the happy pair.

51 "I want to go fishing," said Gary.

"I want to catch lots of fish. I want a fishing rod."

"I want it now!" he shouted at Mum and Dad.

They bought him a rod.

On Saturday Dad took him to the river.

He showed Gary what to do.

"I want a go!" snapped Gary and grabbed the rod.

He cast the line into the river and waited … and waited … and waited.

The other fishermen caught plenty. Gary caught … nothing.

Dad smiled. His plan was working.

When they arrived home, Dad said: "Do you know why you caught no fish?"

Gary shook his head.

"I wanted to give you some bait." said Dad.

"Why didn't you?" said Gary.

"You were too busy telling me what you wanted.

'I want' never gets!"

52 Do you pick on others?

Annie had red hair.

Children shouted: "Ginger nut! Your head's on fire!"

She was upset.

Mrs Jones brought a poster to school.

It had a picture of a family who all had ginger hair.

Underneath it said: 'There are some things in life you can't choose.'

The pupils laughed.

Mrs Jones kept a straight face. She held up a poster of the same family, but someone was missing.

She asked: "Who?"

"The little girl!" shouted the children.

"Can you guess why?" said Mrs Jones.

They couldn't.

She explained: "Sarah was so tired of being picked on, she took her own life."

53	The sale was due to start at 9 o'clock.

People had waited all night for a bargain.

At 8.45am three men knocked over an old lady and pushed in.

Those at the front were too frightened to stop them.

The manager saw what happened.

He opened the doors and said to the men: "What would you like?"

They wanted a digital wide screen TV and a DVD player.

The manager said: "You can have them free with my compliments. I'll put them in a box."

Doubly delighted, they put the box in a van and drove off.

They laughed at the people still queuing.

The manager took the van's number.

He told the police to arrest them.

He said: "You'll find the men opening a box of bricks they haven't paid for."

Everyone gets their just desserts!

54 Do you always work hard?

Ed was the boss. His men were on three sites.

He checked their progress every day.

One gang always worked hard. The others pretended to be busy when they saw Ed coming.

He decided to watch them through a telescope.

He spotted those he couldn't trust.

Ed asked a photographer to take pictures.

One showed a gang smoking and playing cards.

The second group were caught chatting and sunbathing.

The third set of men were working hard.

Ed called a meeting. He said: "There's a bonus for the hardest working group."

A man shouted: "How are you going to decide?"

Ed replied: "I already have."

He showed them the photographs.

After that the threat of the hidden camera kept <u>all</u> the men hard at work.

The Dillon family were on holiday.

Dad cooked tea on the barbecue.

They were about to eat when a young Dutch boy appeared. He said: "Excuse me – can I borrow some charcoal?"

"'Course you can!" answered Dad.

When he'd gone Dad said: "They are good people the Dutch - he'll bring it back."

The boy didn't.

Next morning the children grinned. They said: "You'll never see the charcoal again."

Dad said nothing. At dinner time they giggled: "Thought you could trust the Dutch?"

Dad kept quiet. By the afternoon they really 'rubbed it in'.

They laughed: - "You've no chance. He won't return it!"

Just then - the Dutch boy reappeared.

He brought the charcoal, and gave Dad some chocolate and biscuits to say thank you.

Dad had the last laugh.

His trust was more than repaid.

56 It was bonfire night.

Danny whirled his sparkler.

Dad lit the fireworks.

One didn't set off.

Mum called: "Supper!"

Everyone went in except Danny.

He returned to the firework. He leaned over to see what was wrong.

It burst into flames and burnt his hand badly.

He had to have a false one fitted.

The children at school had never seen anything like it.

They thought it was a toy.

Danny wanted to show them what it was <u>really</u> like.

He took off the hand and said: "I can't feel anything - I am disabled FOR LIFE!"

57

Jason was a 'safe cracker.'

The police had never caught him.

He heard an emergency on the news.

A bank manager was trapped in a vault.

She didn't like tight spaces.

She found it difficult to breathe.

The locksmith was on holiday – no one could open the door.

Jason sped to the bank.

He cracked the code.

The manager was taken to hospital. She suffered from shock.

For the first time Jason had put his skills to good use.

He felt proud instead of guilty.

Jason never 'cracked' another safe.

58 Sometimes churches have a message outside.

This is called a 'Wayside Pulpit.'

One Spring a Vicar organised a competition.

There was a prize for the best new message.

The winner would be announced on Easter Sunday.

Suzy's entry showed a table with three things on:-

A block of butter with 'Jesus is Risen!' written in it.

A knife.

A round slice of half-buttered toast.

Underneath Suzy had put:-

'Go out and be a knife.'

"We can't have that," said the Vicar. "We don't want anyone going out stabbing people."

"It's a table knife!" sobbed Suzy. "I want people to SPREAD THE GOOD NEWS TO ALL THE WORLD."

The Vicar said: "I've heard of disciples going out, missionaries too. Never a knife but there's always a first time."

Suzy won a special prize for a message with a difference!

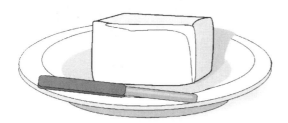

**BE LIKE
A KNIFE**

59

Two boys whispered horrible things about their friends.

It upset them.

Mr Allison made a secret plan with Jenny and Stuart.

He stood his class in two lines.

Jenny was last in the first line.

Stuart the final person in the second.

Mr Allison started two 'Chinese Whispers.'

'She sells sea shells on the sea shore, She sells sea shells'

'Red lorry, yellow lorry, red lorry, yellow lorry…'

When the first whisper reached Jenny she shouted: "Toby has a big nose!"

Stuart then chanted: "Josh's ears stick out!"

It was the boys' turn to be upset.

Mr Allison had told Jenny and Stuart to make the nasty comments.

It gave the boys a taste of their own medicine.

It cured them!

She sells sea shells on the sea ....

Red lorry, Yellow lorry, Red .....

60 Everyone in the village was hurt by the news.

The valley was to be flooded to create a new dam.

Their houses would be drowned.

"There's no point protesting," said the people. "Let's take the money and go."

John asked Dad; "Can I write to the Water Board?"

"Waste of time – it's not worth a stamp," moaned Dad.

John did write.

He sent photographs of the happy families.

He drew pictures of where the children played.

'Your dam will destroy all this,' said the letter.

The Water Board took note.

They decided to flood another valley.

The people celebrated.

It <u>was</u> worth a stamp!

61 Graham got ready for school.

Mum had bought him a new satchel.

He didn't take it.

It wouldn't be cool.

He thought the big boys would tease him on his first day.

Graham was given lots of books to take home.

"Bring them back by tomorrow!" said Mr Gray.

At home-time he piled up the books. They were not easy to balance.

On the way home he dropped them.

One of the older boys came up to him.

Graham expected to be teased and laughed at.

The boy picked up most of the books. He gave the others to Graham.

"I'll help you carry them home" he said.

Graham was pleased to be wrong!

62 The forest animals shouted at Mr Owl.

"You're useless. You stand on a branch and do nothing."

One night a pack of wolves howled.

The animals were frightened.

They called a meeting: "Who's going to warn us if they attack?"

"Not me," said Mr Badger.

"I daren't," said Mr Rabbit.

A feather dropped from above.

Mr Owl was looking all round for danger.

He could see the wolves clearly in the dark.

He promised to warn them with his hoot.

The animals realised
they <u>needed</u> Mr Owl.

63 The sergeant fired the gun.

Ritchie set off.

His aim – to come first and beat the course record.

He splashed through the water.

He crawled under the cargo net.

Next came the monkey bars, then through the tunnel.

He grabbed the zip line and hurtled to the bottom.

Ritchie heard the cries of friends: "You can do it!"

He swung on the rope and climbed the wall.

Ritchie could see the finish line.

He was sure he'd smash the record.

He heard a shout: "I can't make it!"

It was Macca by the wall.

Ritchie paused: "Break the record – or help Macca over?"

He went back.

They climbed it together and finished the course.

Ritchie received a special award.

It was more precious to him than breaking any record.

64 It's not easy to say "No!"

Three lads were exploring the moors.

They found a cave and went in.

There were drawings of soldiers on the wall.

In the rock pools were shiny pebbles and some old coins.

They came across a strange box.

Perhaps it was full of treasure!

They opened it with trembling hands.

Inside were lots of rude pictures.

The lads were tempted to show them to their friends.

Maybe they could sell them?

Wisely, they closed the box.

It was a matter for the police.

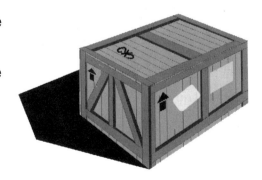

65 Many people are selfish.

They put themselves first.

Donna was the same.

Her word for life was: 'D O G.'

It stood for **D**onna – **O**thers – **G**od.

One night she wanted to go to a disco.

She was short of money.

As she reached to take some from the charity box, she looked in the mirror.

The reflection looked as though she was giving.

It made her realise it should have been the other way round – G O D.

God – **O**thers – **D**onna.

Always put God first, others second and yourself last.

66 The school grounds were full of litter.

The Head Teacher tried everything.

She offered rewards, made threats, sent teams out.

None worked.

She let the litter build up.

Mrs Robinson told the pupils. "I've invited a famous football team. They are going to play a match against us."

The children were excited.

The school team practised hard.

The game was advertised in the local paper.

On match day the Manager inspected the pitch.

In assembly he said; "We can't play on that. The game's cancelled."

"Why?" asked the disappointed children.

"Why do <u>you</u> think?" he said.
He held up a rusty Coke can.

Mrs Robinson's plan had
worked.

67 Do you put things off?

There was a competition on the radio.

"Why don't you phone in?" said Lizzie's Mum. She did.

The presenter said: "Answer 3 questions to win a trip to Disneyland."

Lizzie answered all three correctly.

"You've won!" said the DJ. "Please return the claim form by Friday."

Lizzie filled it in. She said: "I'll post it tomorrow."

The following Monday, she turned the radio on.

The presenter said: "We still have a trip to Disneyland to give away. Last week's winner didn't claim it!"

"I did!" shouted Lizzie.

Mum pointed at the envelope on the sideboard.

It was still waiting to be posted.

Don't put off till tomorrow things you can do today.

68 Two teenagers saw a man begging.

He was sitting with a cap in front of him.

Next to it was a sign. It read: 'Hungry & Homeless.'

The boys watched people dropping coins into the cap.

"What an easy way to make money!" said Robert.

"We could try it," said Chris.

They found a different place. Robert took his baseball cap off.

Chris wrote: 'Starving & Jobless' on piece of cardboard.

They smiled as the cap began to fill.

A Policeman appeared.

He took them to the station for questioning.

They were kept in a cell to wait for their Parents.

"I'm starving. I want to go home." said Robert.

"You've only been here 4 hours!" said the Policeman. "Harry feels like that all the time."

The boys were sorry.

On their way home, they tipped the money into Harry's cap.

HUNGRY & HOMELESS

69 Mr Cole gave marks out of ten for his pupils' work.

He awarded smiley faces for trying hard.

One for average effort. Two for good.

Lisa scored 8's and 9's.

She only got one smiley face.

Trudy's marks were 5's and 6's.

She was given two smiley faces.

Lisa didn't think this was fair.

She watched Trudy working.

While others were talking and messing about, Trudy concentrated.

She was trying her very best.

Lisa thought about her own work.

Her effort didn't match Trudy's.

In her next piece of work she gave maximum effort.

She got 10 out of 10 and 2 smiley faces.

Mr Cole's smiley faces encouraged <u>every</u> pupil to try their very best.

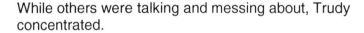

70 Mum got a mobile phone for her birthday.

She learnt to ring and send text messages.

"We'll show you how to use the answer phone," said Adrian.

"I haven't time," she replied.

_____

Mum wanted an MG sports car.

The children went to the newsagents for opening time.

They looked for a bargain.

An advert read: 'MG sports car. Immaculate condition. First to see will buy.'

"Let's ring Mum. She might miss it," said Carol.

They left a message on her answer phone.

Mum never received it.

At tea-time Adrian said; "Did you get our message? We wanted you to be first."

"For what?" Mum replied.

"A bargain MG sports car!"

"No, I'll ring now."

The first to see did buy.

It could have been Mum.

71 Pundaz lived in India.

He loved his two elephants Toza and Mila.

One day hunters trapped Toza! They took him away in a cage.

He was to be shot for his ivory tusks.

Pundaz followed the men with Mila. Their house was next to a pond.

He let Mila have a long drink.

Pundaz tapped on the door.

When the men appeared he gave Mila a signal.

The elephant squirted water at them from his trunk.

It knocked them over. Pundaz snatched the keys.

Toza was set free.

On the way home a deadly snake crawled towards Pundaz.

It was Toza's turn to save his master.

He tossed the snake away with one of his tusks.

Tusks are valuable in more ways than one.

72 Mr Brunswick lived by himself.

He enjoyed spending time in the garden.

Neighbours asked questions.

They meant well. He thought they were nosy.

He built a high wall to keep them out.

Boys climbed up it.

He made it even higher.
It looked like a castle.

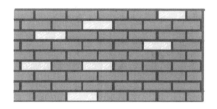

For a while Mr Brunswick
was happy.

During Winter it became dark, quiet and lonely.

He'd cut off the outside world.

Mr Brunswick didn't like it. He removed a brick.

He heard children playing.

Birds were singing, trees budding, flowers blooming.

He was glad to see them.

Mr Brunswick knocked the wall down.

The bricks were used to build a new community centre.

He held an 'open house' party for his neighbours.

They were pleased to join him.

73 Have you ever been in hospital?

Anisah needed an operation.

Her doctor came to tell her about it.

She was frightened.

The nurses talked to her. She was still scared.

The surgeon came. He showed her what he was going to do.

Anisah didn't sleep that night.

Raymond was the 'trolley boy'.

He took her to the operating theatre.

She was crying.

Raymond leaned over and said: "Your Mum says you like painting. I'll get you some paper and paint when you come out".

Anisah smiled. She was no longer afraid.

Three weeks later, Raymond received a parcel.

Inside was a painting of Anisah's smiling face.

A card said: 'Thank you for putting me at ease'.

Raymond pinned them to the side of his trolley.

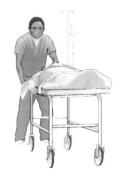

74 There were 2 cyber cafés * in town.

One was busy, the other quiet.

Mr Pearson, the manager of the quiet café was puzzled.

He said to one of his workers: "Why are all the children going there? Go and find out!"

He reported: "Everyone kept looking at a big clock".

The manager bought an even bigger one for his café.

It didn't make any difference.

"Go and ask the children why?" said the owner.

They told the worker: "Mr Hughes gives us an extra 5 – 10 minutes. Mr Pearson kicks us out on the hour!"

When he heard this, Mr Pearson said: "Why is the big clock so special if time doesn't matter?"

The worker said: "The children told me it helps them not to take advantage of Mr Hughes' generosity".

The clock was a symbol of trust.

(*Footnote:- At a cyber café you can surf the net and buy refreshments.)

75 Can you be trusted?

The netball team trained hard all season.

They reached the semi-final of the cup.

Miss Taylor was delighted when her team scored a last minute winner.

They were in the final!

She felt proud.

When they got back to school Miss Taylor rang the head teacher; "Mr Simpson – We won!"

When she'd gone, the players took a lollipop from Mrs Crossley's jar.

Next day a team member owned up.

Miss Taylor was ashamed to report the theft.

She felt the team should be punished by missing the final.

Mr Simpson agreed. He spoke to the girls: "You've stolen lollipops and robbed Miss Taylor of her pride. After all she's given, you have betrayed her trust. The reserves will play the final!"

Robbed of her pride.

| 76 | The graveyard was a mess.

Vandals broke headstones. |

They wrote graffiti and trampled on flowers.

Jamie was the worst.

He threw stones, dropped rubbish and ran between graves.

Jamie saw one with a white cross on top.

He smashed it to pieces.

Later a visitor tapped him on the shoulder.

"I'm Uncle Peter. You won't remember me.

I can't find the grave with a white cross on top."

Jamie smirked and pointed to the broken stones.

His uncle pieced them together.

He called Jamie over and showed him the words:-

'In memory of Nellie, devoted wife of John, much-loved mother of Peter and Arthur, loving grandmother of Paula, Dean and …… JAMIE.'

77 One day a Vicar came into a church. He held two Bibles in front of the children.

The first was brand new. Its cover gleamed. The other was old. It was dull, tattered and torn.

The Vicar asked the children: "Which do you think is the best bible?" They pointed to the new one.

After a few seconds silence, the Vicar exclaimed: "But nobody's ever read that one! Its pages haven't been opened. How can it be the best? It has never done any good!"

He held up the old Bible again. "This has been read by hundreds of boys and girls. They have read the stories of Jesus lots of times. They have remembered them and learned to live their lives as He did."

Every book including the Bible is meant to be read, enjoyed and remembered.

78 Every month the school had a fire drill.

When the alarm bell rang each class went into the playground. The teacher told them to remain quiet and calm and took the register.

Some children said: "It's not a real fire, it's only a drill!" They pushed and pulled each other as they went out. They laughed and talked during the register.

The teacher pointed out their behaviour meant it took twice as long to leave safely.

They replied: "What difference does a minute or two make?"

The teacher built a paper tower and put it in a metal tray. She struck a match and set it on fire.

It was ablaze in seconds. Within two minutes it burnt to the ground.

The children were shocked.

The extra two minutes could have cost them their lives.

79 Gupta was an Egyptian guide.

Every day he led tourists up one of the Great Pyramids. He charged a fee and some holiday makers gave him a tip.

Gupta thought of a greedy trick. He got a friend to come with the party. He asked him to puff and pant loudly when they stopped halfway.

"It's tiring!" said Gupta. "There's no need to go to the top. The view is just as good here."

The people didn't like to argue. They followed him back without complaining.

Gupta took twice as many parties up the pyramid. He doubled his wages.

It might have served him right if he had fallen off the pyramid. The Bible says: - 'The wages of sin is death.'

Gupta laughed at his friends. He did half the work for double their wage. They soon wiped the smile off his face. They offered half price trips to the top.

Twice as many people went with them!

80 An express train sped down the line at 100mph. It hurtled past a red light and ploughed into a stationary goods train. 120 people were killed. Many others were injured.

The newspapers looked for someone to blame. Was it the driver's fault? The signalman? Teenage vandals?

How could such a tragic accident occur?

Why did God let it happen?

The investigation team found a red brick office had been built behind the signal. They could not see the red light against a background of the same colour. No wonder the driver had missed it – especially driving at a high speed.

The signal was re-sited where it could be seen clearly.

Nobody likes to see accidents happen, but each time we learn from them our world becomes a safer place to live in.

81

On holiday in Fiji we visited a museum.

We read about people being boiled alive. It carried on until English missionaries came to the Islands in the 19th century. They stopped the evil killing by bringing the message of Jesus.

In the middle of our trip we had a flat tyre on a lonely road. As I struggled to jack up the car, three huge Fijians ran out from the bushes! I was frightened.

They quickly changed the wheel, shook my hand and waved goodbye with a proud smile on their face. I didn't realise until we got to the garage they'd also put a box of pineapples in the boot.

Just think. One hundred and fifty years ago, we'd have been in the pot !

People can change!

82 Andrew trained to be a Vicar. His first job was to speak in a prison! He had no idea what to talk about. He was so nervous he tripped on the stairs to the platform. He fell to the bottom.

The prisoners laughed. He was down in more ways than one.

Bravely he picked himself up. Now he knew what to say!

"When I was down, I could have felt sorry for myself and walked out – You must feel down. You know you've done wrong. You have lost your freedom. Who's going to lift you up?

"YOU have to pick yourself up – like I did. Start to rebuild your life like I'm restarting my talk".

It was one of the best talks Andrew gave.

Everyone listened.

83 We used to play a special game in the school gym.

The teacher put a mat out. She challenged us to get as many boys and girls on as possible. When someone fell on the floor, our score would be the number of children left on the mat.

It was easy in the middle. The real test was for those on the outside. They had to let others squash on the edge and keep hold of them. The best teams were prepared to put up with discomfort and make room for another.

Twelve farm workers were potato-picking. Suddenly a storm broke.

They ran for cover in a tiny church. Eleven of them piled in. The last one tried to squeeze in out of the rain. The others wouldn't let him. They shouted angrily; "There's no room for you!" They pushed him over on to the muddy field and slammed the church door.

Ten seconds later, there was a clap of thunder. A bolt of lightening struck the church tower. It collapsed crushing the workers to death.

If they'd made room for him, maybe it wouldn't have happened.

84 When you get on a bus you pay the driver your fare.

Money used to be collected by a bus conductor.

One day at a seaside town, two old ladies boarded a bus. They asked the conductor for two tickets to the South Pier. He politely told them they'd got on the wrong bus. This one was going to the North Pier!

The ladies couldn't hear very well. They asked again for the South Pier. The conductor remained patient. He tried to make it clear the bus was going in the opposite direction. He pointed the other way to help them understand. Still the ladies insisted they wanted tickets to the South.

The conductor kept calm. He smiled at them, then rang the bell to stop the bus. He guided the ladies off and led them safely across the road. He waved a Southbound bus to a halt and helped them find a seat.

The passengers on the first bus were kept waiting. They were late. When the conductor returned he expected them to be angry. Everyone smiled as they stood to give him a big clap.

His patience was rewarded.

85 Mum chatted to her school teacher friend who was upset about her class. Some children drank two bottles of milk instead of one. They were greedy.

Mum wanted to stop her family being like this.

She gave her children 3 parcels - small, medium and large. Each had a surprise in.

They had to choose one.

All four chose the big parcel - but the best present was in the smallest!

Next she gave 3 money envelopes. One was thick. Another medium. The last slim.

All four opened the thick envelope. It contained lots of Monopoly money! The second was full of blank cheques. The third had a ten pound note inside.

The children realised Mum was trying to teach them a lesson.

She gave each four tins. A small light tin up to a large heavy tin. They were asked to keep one.

Each kept the small tin and gave the larger ones away.

Mum said: "You don't need to open them".

"Why not?" they said.

"You've passed the test."

They had learnt not to be greedy.

86 Susan was having tea with her family. Suddenly a group of soldiers burst into the house. The sergeant shouted: "Line them up against the wall – all except the girl, she's mine!"

She watched in horror as her parents and brother were shot. The sergeant took her away. He did cruel things to her.

Luckily she managed to escape. She became a nurse in a military hospital.

Six months later a badly wounded soldier was brought in. It was the sergeant!

Susan wanted revenge for her family. She could shoot him or leave him to bleed to death.

Susan didn't abandon him. She nursed him back to health.

When he opened his eyes he recognised her immediately. He asked: "Why have you looked after me?"

She replied: "My parents taught me to forgive".

When was the last time you forgave somebody?

87 Ants work together.

They follow in line and collect food for their family.

Mr Bateman worked for the National Children's Home.

He challenged Bilbury Primary School to raise £1000 in 4 weeks.

Pupils planned fun runs. They had a summer fair. Teachers had wet sponges thrown at them.

A month passed. The money was collected.

The amount was announced in Assembly - £995.50

Larry went red. He hadn't bothered to collect his sponsor money.

He'd let the school down.

Success comes when we work as a team!

88 Mike was a stuntman.

When dangerous scenes were filmed he took the star's place. He did jumps, climbs and dives to escape from crashes, traps, explosions and floods.

It was Mike's last day before retiring. He was filming the final reel of an action movie.

Suddenly he heard someone screaming! It was a young girl. She had swam out of her depth at the bottom of a cliff. By the time anyone climbed to help she would drown. Mike didn't hesitate. He dived off the cliff – a huge drop of 200m into the waves.

With great skill and courage he pulled her to safety.

On his last day Mike performed his most spectacular stunt. He risked his life to save the girl's.

No one will forget Mike's dive.

It's a pity the cameras weren't rolling.

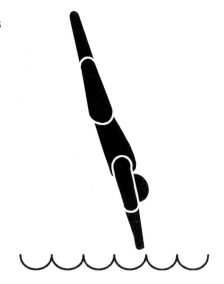

| 89 | Jesus told a story. A woman put a small coin in a collection box. It was everything she had. |

A young boy gave all he had - 5 loaves and two fishes. It helped feed 5,000 people.

Decko the clown felt ashamed when he saw people giving money to Jesus. He didn't have any.

At midnight he took his coloured objects and began to juggle them in front of the church altar. A man was upset by this, and he told the Vicar.

The Vicar came to see what was going on. He smiled and said: "Decko is offering all he has – his juggling skills".

What can you give?

90 A man was riding his horse. He stopped where some soldiers were mending a wall.

It kept falling down in front of their corporal.

"They could do with your help!" said the rider.

"Corporals don't build walls," he replied.

The man got off his horse and rolled up his sleeves. He helped the soldiers lift the heavy stones. The wall was soon finished.

They thanked him.

He said to the corporal: "Don't forget to write in your report - the General was pleased to help!"

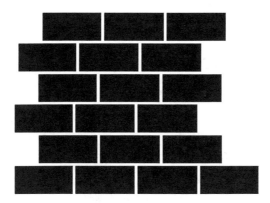

91 Are you happy?

Tom wasn't. He didn't want to work. He said: "I'd like to be a bird and fly to different places".

Shortly afterwards, Tom had a dream. He was a bird.

He was surprised he had nowhere to sleep. He had to build a nest.

He didn't have any food or money to buy some. He had to find something to eat.

He had nothing to drink. He had to search for a stream and wash in dirty puddles.

One day he was chased by a cat, and shot at by a cruel boy.

When it was cold other birds knew where to go. They left to warmer countries.

Tom followed. He was very tired after flying thousands of miles.

When the alarm clock woke him, Tom was glad he wasn't a bird.

He was content with what he had. Are you?

| **92** | An artist was asked to paint pictures for a new Bible. |

He needed a person who looked like Jesus. He searched for someone kind, honest, gentle, caring and loving.

He found a man and paid him to model as Jesus.

During the next 2 years he asked men and women to pose for different people in the Bible.

His last picture was about Jesus being tempted by the Devil.

He looked everywhere for someone with an evil, cunning and hateful face. He found a man in a dirty place for the homeless and unemployed.

The artist offered him money to model the Devil. He began to cry. "What's the matter?" said the artist.

The man replied: - "You don't recognise me… I'm the same person you paid to model Jesus 2 years ago…. My life has gone downhill. I now look like the Devil."

It's a pity this story isn't the other way round – an evil man becoming good enough to be like Jesus.

93

Jake was a robber.

One night he broke into a warehouse and stole £10,000 from the safe. On his way out he tripped and set the alarm off.

The security guard saw Jake and chased him across the yard.

When they came to a barbed wire fence, Jake climbed safely over.

The guard was caught in the wire and cut his arms and legs badly. As Jake escaped down the road, the man shouted: "Help! Help! I've hurt myself. I'm bleeding".

Jake stopped. Should he risk being caught?

He went back and cut the guard free. He bound his wounds and rang for an ambulance.

In the meantime the alarm had alerted the police. Jake was arrested.

When he was sentenced, the judge took into account his decision to help the guard.

There is some good in everybody.

94

When I was a young boy, Dad cooked my breakfast every day.

I loved the smell of bacon and egg when I walked into the kitchen. The plate of food was always on the table, warm and ready to eat.

One day some tiles blew off our house roof.

Dad needed to replace them quickly because it was starting to rain.

He bought 6 new tiles and fetched the ladder from the shed. He said: "Son, hold the ladder please – make sure I don't fall!"

I replied: "I've got to go Dad, football practice is in 10 minutes – ask Mum".

The next morning there was no smell of bacon and eggs.

My plate was there with a note. It read 'Penalty for not holding ladder for Dad – one breakfast.'

95 Pop groups go on tour. They take lots of equipment with them.

People called 'roadies' set it up. They carry things on stage and make sure everything is safe.

They are treated as important members of the team.

Church organs used to be pumped by a helper. He pedalled bellows or pumped a handle which provided air for the pipes and meant the organ could play.

One Sunday an organist boasted to people in church: "Didn't I do well?"

The week after his organ wouldn't play. The man on the bellows stayed at home.

From then on the organist never forgot to thank him and always said: "Didn't WE do well?"

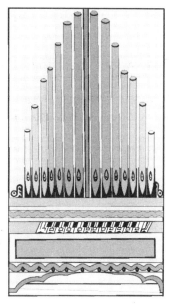

96 Mum came home and slammed the door.

She walked into the kitchen. It was a tip.

The dishwasher hadn't been emptied. Dirty cups and saucers were everywhere. The bin was overflowing. The cat hadn't been fed.

She was furious. She shouted: "I've had enough. I'm not doing it!"

Mum fell asleep.

Later she heard a crash in the kitchen.

She stormed in. A cup was smashed to pieces on the floor.

She went mad; "Suzy, get upstairs to bed. That's one of my favourite cups."

Suzy went to her room upset.

It wasn't until later, Mum realised Suzy had cleaned and tidied the kitchen. It was spotless.

The sound she'd heard was the last cup being broken.

Mum wished she'd stopped to think before losing her temper.

97 Mobile phones are useful.

They can be used for emergencies and ringing family and friends.

Carrie moved school. She was happy at first.

She used her mobile to ring old mates.

Pupils at her new school asked for her number.

Her first calls were funny and friendly.

One day she received a text message. It read: 'We don't like you – you don't fit in here!'

Carrie was upset.

Her class mates were using their phones to bully her.

The headmaster was angry when he heard. He banned mobiles from school.

In Assembly he held a sign with a BT logo. It read: 'It's good to talk.'

Underneath it said: **'ONLY** if you've got something <u>good</u> to say!'

98 Haythorpe School had a 'Big Brother' competition.

Video cameras recorded 5 children in a classroom for a day.

The rest of the school voted out one child every hour.

Michael said nothing – he went first.

Second was Ayishah - she never smiled.

Peter followed because of his bad language.

Jenny went fourth, she was selfish.

Gavin was the winner. He told jokes and made everyone laugh.

The Head Teacher gave him his prize.

Next day Mr McKenzie replayed the video.

He asked the children to watch Michael carefully.

They saw him share his sweets, comfort Ayishah, and feed the cat.

The children realised Michael was the real 'Big Brother!'

99 Kelly and Helen made fun of Teresa; "We can beat you at anything," they teased.

The three girls entered the 'Tall Trees Trek' - a race into the middle of a thick forest and back.

They were allowed to take one thing to help.

Kelly took a compass.

Helen chose a map.

Teresa thought for a while, then filled a bag with white pebbles.

At the start line, Helen and Kelly laughed at Teresa; "What use is that?" they said, pointing at the bag.

Helen and Kelly raced off. They didn't see Teresa cut a small hole in the bag.

The two girls reached the centre of the forest long before Teresa.

It was getting dark as they turned round.

They found it difficult to read their compass and map. They were soon lost.

By the time Teresa reached the middle, her bag was empty.

She followed the white pebbles all the way back.

A group of friends were surprised to see her return first.

Teresa's trail helped her to win, and guided a rescue team to find Helen and Kelly.

They never laughed at Teresa again.

100 Class 4 had a mental maths test every Friday.

Matt and Kev usually scored 5 out of ten.

After a few weeks they began to get full marks.

Miss Simpson was suspicious.

She separated the two boys.

They still managed to get 10 out of 10.

The class became annoyed.

One Friday, Tina saw the boys take the answer sheet from inside Miss Simpson's book. They copied them and put it back.

She reported them.

The following week, Miss Simpson planted a special set of answers in the book for Matt and Kev.

They fell for the trap.

Before the next test, she sent them on an errand.

Whilst they were gone, Miss Simpson gave the <u>right</u> answers to the rest of the class.

Everyone scored 10 out of 10 except Matt and Kev!

MOORLEY'S

We are growing publishers, adding several new titles to our list each year. We also undertake private publications and commissioned works.

Our range of publications includes:

Books of Verse:
Devotional Poetry
Recitations
Drama
Bible Plays
Sketches
Nativity Plays
Passiontide Plays
Easter Plays
Demonstrations
Resource Books
Assembly Material
Songs and Musicals
Children's Addresses
Prayers and Graces
Daily Readings
Books for Speakers
Activity Books
Quizzes
Puzzles
Painting Books
Church Stationery
Notice Books
Cradle Rolls
Hymn Board Numbers

Please send a stamped addressed envelope (approx. 9" x 6") for the current catalogue or consult your local Christian Bookshop who should stock or be able to order our titles.